# SEVEN SUNS / SEVEN MOONS

Michael Dylan Welch & Tanya McDonald

NeoPoiesisPress.com

NeoPoiesis Press, LLC

2775 Harbor Ave SW, Suite D, Seattle, WA 98126-2138
Inquiries: Info@NeoPoiesisPress.com
NeoPoiesisPress.com

Some of these poems previously appeared in *Roadrunner*.

Seven Suns / Seven Moons
ISBN  978-0-9903565-9-2 (pbk)

    1. Poetry. I. Welch, Michael Dylan. II. McDonald, Tanya.

Library of Congress Control Number: 2016949831

First Edition

Printed in the United States of America.

# Contents

## Seven Suns

## Seven Moons

❂

# Seven Suns

Michael Dylan Welch

## Prelude

one sun

rising over the rooftops

to the west

two suns

a reflection

of my icy self

three suns

phases of geometry

in her bones

four suns

the gear shift

loud to my touch

five suns
the wrench floats
in our common dream


six suns
from here to there
a broken path


seven suns
raindrops about to hit
the cracked windshield

# One

seven suns
a bridge to somewhere
in the fog

seven suns
we talk awhile
of foreign politics

seven suns
for some the snowfall
is a delight

seven suns
my speed over the limit
on the digital roadside sign

seven suns
a past life
opens the door


seven suns
the bell tolls
for the firefighter


seven suns
disjunction
on a sycamore leaf

# Two

seven suns

Nostradamus

eats my eye


seven suns

the penis

mightier than the sword


seven suns

in the woods we go the way

of the dinosaur


seven suns

few have known

the taste of demons

seven suns
the invoice sent
straight to heaven

seven suns
the word processor
corrects my spelling

seven suns
a trace of pesticide
on this apple

# Three

seven suns

the colour pink

drones into clouds


seven suns

paper for recycling

made into a hat


seven suns

the soccer ball floats

over the goal


seven suns

the customs agent

restamps my passport

seven suns

lowering into the pond

Easter Sunday


seven suns

a registered charity

files for bankruptcy


seven suns

the necessity

of comparison

# Four

seven suns
the hollow in your dream
filled with eyes

seven suns
the nun at the corner
dances a jig

seven suns
the recommendation letter
I never wanted

seven suns
the travel agent
asks me my name

seven suns
the sermon today
on abstinence


seven suns
together we polish
our paragraphs


seven suns
gang members laughing
at a comic strip

# Five

seven suns
the pornography
of bird-watching

seven suns
the Loch Ness monster
knows my name

seven suns
the spare tire
also flat

seven suns
my emotion
goes out on a date

seven suns

for once I'm not asked

if I want fries with that


seven suns

the coupon I used

had expired


seven sons

each one

by a different father

# Six

seven suns

inflatable pools

now half price


seven suns

the pregnant woman

sighs again


seven suns

the song on the radio

receding with my hairline


seven suns

her fart

in the elevator

seven suns
Godzilla attacks
Topeka

seven suns
the in-flight movie
ended early for landing

seven suns
the software works
exactly as advertised

# Seven

seven suns
my keys dropped
down a gopher hole

seven suns
the ski report says
watch for rocks

seven suns
the neighbourhood cinema
closed for remodeling

seven suns
balcony tomato plants
about to ripen

seven suns
this taxi driver
untalkative

seven suns
the teacher's face
looks explosive

seven suns
the first-class stamp
insufficient

# Postlude

seven suns

he tells me they use

the rhythm method


six suns

her pendant swings

into the salad


five suns

the bishop's case

dismissed


four suns

a sudden flurry

of typing

three suns

she plugs in her iPod

for recharging


two puns

the laughter

you never gave me


one sun

setting below the rooftops

in the east

# Seven Moons

*Tanya McDonald*

# Prelude

*one moon*
*counting pennies*
*in a jar*

*two moons*
*the wrinkled bedspread*
*where he sat*

*three moons*
*last week's cheese*
*turning blue*

*four moons*
*the globe from my childhood*
*out of date*

*five moons*
*Ophelia bathes*
*with wildflowers*

*six moons*
*an empty vase*
*on the mantle*

*seven moons*
*no mountains visible*
*today*

# One

*seven moons*
*frying up mushrooms*
*for lunch*

*seven moons*
*the hens content*
*not to lay*

*seven moons*
*ducks fly*
*at the train's passing*

*seven moons*
*a cat allergy*
*keeps him from visiting*

*seven moons*

*tasting the cookie dough*

*one more time*


*seven moons*

*according to her gravestone*

*she hasn't died*


*seven moons*

*the phone number*

*he never gave me*

# Two

*seven moons*
*the fireplace boarded up*
*on Christmas Eve*

*seven moons*
*a slate-colored junco*
*matches the sky*

*seven moons*
*shelves collecting books*
*and dust*

*seven moons*
*we discuss financing*
*for our first house*

*seven moons*

*the boy in the manga*

*winks at me*


*seven moons*

*a broken spoke*

*on the umbrella*


*seven moons*

*the cat uncurls*

*into a crescent*

# Three

*seven moons*
*skinny-dipping*
*in the sea*

*seven moons*
*the green dragon points*
*northwest*

*seven moons*
*I always wanted*
*glasses*

*seven moons*
*an afternoon spent*
*in the gardening section*

*seven moons*

*she flings spaghetti noodles*

*at the wall*


*seven moons*

*under the bed I find*

*my marbles*


*seven moons*

*the cat that Mom*

*ran over*

# Four

*seven moons*

*sneaking down to the beach*

*for sex*

*seven moons*

*the asparagus*

*too tough to eat*

*seven moons*

*between showers*

*the thrush's whistle*

*seven moons*

*once I enjoyed the taste*

*of rum & Cokes*

*seven moons*

*the rattle*

*of the beer can's widget*


*seven moons*

*the bicycle I lusted after*

*sold*


*seven moons*

*tucked in a drawer*

*unworn baby socks*

# Five

*seven moons*

*he brings binoculars*

*to the soccer match*


*seven moons*

*upon reaching the highlands*

*he passes a bottle of whisky*


*seven moons*

*the wedding photographer*

*changes my flat tire*


*seven suns*

*my high school crush*

*in my dreams again*

*seven moons*

*blues and the news*

*at the sushi bar*


*seven moons*

*the shopping list*

*includes condoms*


*seven moons*

*my juror number*

*not chosen*

# Six

*seven moons*
*I pretend I'm not*
*at home*

*seven moons*
*the vampire gets*
*a cavity*

*seven moons*
*the cat now minus*
*a whisker*

*seven moons*
*my birthday card arrives*
*postage due*

*seven moons*

*they make love*

*in sigh language*


*seven moons*

*during the season finale*

*I drop a stitch*


*seven moons*

*the smiling Care Bears*

*say nothing*

# Seven

*seven moons*

*chipped blue paint*

*on the bonsai pot*


*seven moons*

*yesterday's plane crash*

*attributed to ice*


*seven moons*

*following his boot tread*

*back to camp*


*seven moons*

*an army of earthworms*

*beached on the sidewalk*

*seven moons*

*he asks if anyone has lost*

*a credit card*


*seven moons*

*a pale scar*

*from the rooster's beak*


*seven moons*

*he keeps my four-leaf clover*

*in his wallet*

# Postlude

*seven moons*
*an alarm goes off*
*on my biological clock*

*six moons*
*a thermos of green tea*
*on the counter*

*five moons*
*an origami frog*
*watches the rain*

*four moons*
*I receive an appraisal*
*of her diamond ring*

*three moons*

*two sisters*

*one room*


*two loons*

*snowbound*

*on our anniversary*


*one moon*

*the poem he left*

*in my tip jar*

# High Score

seven suns
the economy
of childhood

*seven suns*
*the vending machine jammed*

counting them all
more than seven suns
in the dragonfly's eye

*reflecting on the necklace*

*of the Puget Sound mermaid*

*seven suns*


all that jazz

and seven suns


*seven suns*

*the high score on the arcade game*

*is my phone number*

# Torpedo

*seven moons*

*eating ginger candy*

*as the ferry sways*

seven moonies

at the check-in counter

*right on time*

*the wayward grebe sinks*

*all seven moons*

seven moons

the rising tide

of immigrants


*the pinball machine gives me*

*seven new moons*


seven moons

for the misbegotten

a torpedo on its way

# Up

first warm day
seven suns
are not enough

> *seven moons*
> *peer over the eaves*

seven suns
the new immigrant
conjugates a verb

> *wrapped in a frayed quilt*
> *all seven moons*

the fifth

of the seven suns

eclipsed


*seven moons*

*short a piece of silver*


*the treasure*

*hidden inside an egg*

*seven suns*


playing golf

on the seventh moon


*do you like butter?*

*she holds seven suns*

*to his chin*

seven moons

he pours her wine


*seven suns*

*the digits*

*of this phone number*


once upon a time

seven moons


*lost in the weave*

*of a plaid slipper*

*seven suns*


at the juvie center

seven moons

*the baby shakes*

*the seven suns*

*to pieces*

    sevenmoonlight

    on the surgery scar

*seven suns*

*the black hen*

*eats another blossom*

    my head shrunken

    by the seven moons

seven suns

our tickets booked

to Mazatlan

*the sandcastle holds*

*seven honeymoons*

arctic wind

seven suns

for seven brothers

*after the earthquake*

*seven silent moons*

the butcher knife

stuck in the cheese rind

seven suns

*seven moons*

*what's in a name?*

a sun is a sun

is a sun is a sun is a sun

is a sun is a sun


    *thistle seeds*

    *scattering the seven moons*


sevensunburned

the stranded pod

of pilot whales


    *circulating the petition*

    *seven moons*


seven suns

the time it takes

to say I'm jobless

*carousel horse nodding*

*to the tune of seven moons*

*empty stadium*

*a hummingbird feeds*

*on seven sunsets*

seven moons

since we met

*grinding the last*

*seven suns of coffee*

*for the unexpected guest*

added to my star chart

seven moons

*seven suns*

*strung among the leis*

*around his neck*

    up up and away

    to the seven moons

## Courting the Eyeball Kick:
## A Short History of Suns and Moons

"We all shine on, like the moon, and the stars, and the sun."
—*John Lennon*

Driven by an idea and a seven-fold structure, I wrote the original sixty-three verses for "Seven Suns" over the course of two days. Tanya McDonald's "Seven Moons" verses, inspired by reading "Seven Suns," were a brilliant expansion of the original concept. We decided to try writing more, producing the "Up" renku, and the "High Score" and "Torpedo" rengay.

The "Seven Suns" poems arose partly as an extension of my neon buddha series, writing many poems with that repeated phrase as a sort of personal mythology. They also arose from Allen Ginsberg's concept of the "eyeball kick," which he employed with the phrase "hydrogen jukebox" in *Howl*. My thought was to pick a double-take phrase that wasn't quite true, thus a little surreal, and juxtapose each use of that phrase with a (usually) concrete image, ringing the changes as the poems went along. The juxtapositions aren't quite random. And yet, as the verses shift, exploring the everyday in deliberately leaping ways, a poetic energy bubbles and boils in the seemingly haphazard pairing of each image. The same energy emerges in Tanya's "Seven Moons." Some verses even have a science fiction vibe to them.

The idea behind the "eyeball kick" is not just Ginsberg's of course, since Ginsberg partially got it from haiku. Haiku has employed such juxtaposition for centuries. The term "eyeball kick" has also been attributed online to science fiction writer Rudy Rucker, who has described it as "A perfect, telling detail that creates an instant and powerful visual image." That's a fitting description of haiku, but I think Ginsberg's use of the term predates any association it may have with Rucker. Ginsberg expanded on the idea in his longer poetry by using repeated pairings of unexpected images and phrases.

This juxtapositional technique also came from Ginsberg's study of Paul Cézanne in 1948–49. In *Cézanne: A Life* (Pantheon, 2012), biographer Alex Danchev explains that Ginsberg noticed "a strange shuddering impression looking at his [Cézanne's] canvasses . . . a sudden shift, a flashing" that he called "eyeball kicks." Danchev says that Ginsberg "sought a verbal equivalent," and that his "favorite example was 'hydrogen jukebox.'" In a *Paris Review* interview (#37, Spring 1966), Ginsberg says "I had the idea, perhaps overrefined, that by the unexplainable, unexplained nonperspective line, that is, juxtaposition of one word against another . . . there'd be a gap between two words that the mind would fill in with the sensation of existence. . . . Or in haiku, you have two distinct images, set side by side without drawing a . . . logical connection." Thus, in his own poetry, inspired by haiku and Cézanne, Ginsberg combined high culture with low, the strong with the weak, and the holy with the unholy. This created what Ginsberg called "an electrochemical effect."

I was pleased that Tanya had responded to my verses in such an engaged fashion, but more than that, it fascinated me that some sort of energy in what I had written had caught fire in what she wrote in response. Tanya's idea to jump from the sun to the moon added yin to my yang, night to my day—the pairing of the two parts itself like an eyeball kick. For both of us, the process was swift and spontaneous. Perhaps we tapped into what Charles Olson referred to when he defined poetry itself as a transfer of energy.

The repeated phrases we used provide an obvious link from verse to verse, but we also sought to "taste all of life" the way renku does, as each verse constantly shifts away. "The moon and the sun," as Bashō said, "are eternal travelers." This technique informs the relationship of verses not just in the "Up" renku but also within the "Seven Suns" and "Seven Moons" sequences, and in the two rengay. However, I was not trying to link the verses at all, and tried my best to avoid that, other than with the repeated phrase. Tanya mirrored that stance in her verses. In contrast, we trust readers will find an added synergy in the riffs and relationships, verse by verse, between each successive verse in the "Seven Suns" section when compared with its counterpart in "Seven Moons."

While the poems in this book are not necessarily haiku, they are perhaps on its fringe, and we came at them with haiku minds, minds both steeped in that tradition and open to variation and possibility. We hope readers will catch the energy that ended up suffusing our exploration of each sun and moon verse. Embrace the eyeball kick—and don't blink!

—*Michael Dylan Welch*

# About the Authors

**Michael Dylan Welch** lives in Sammamish, Washington. When he isn't writing, he likes to ski, play racquetball, hike, take photographs, plan outings with his wife and two children, build his music library of great guitar solos, read books, and tend to his website at www.graceguts.com. Michael is especially active with haiku poetry, and he's published his writing and translations in dozens of books and hundreds of journals and anthologies in at least twenty languages, including on the back of 150,000,000 U.S. postage stamps.

**Tanya McDonald** is known for her love of haiku, chickens, and bird-watching. Fond of wearing bright colors and drinking tea, she lives with her husband and their orange cat in a house full of books in Woodinville, Washington. An active member of Haiku Northwest, she was one of eighteen poets featured in *A New Resonance 7*, and was one of four featured readers at the twenty-fifth annual Two Autumns haiku reading in San Francisco. When she's not writing haiku, she's busy working on a trio of young adult novels set in the Seattle area.

## NeoPoiesis: *a new way of making*

1) in ancient Greece, poiesis referred to the process of making: creation - production - organization - formation - causation

2) a process that can be physical and spiritual, biological and intellectual, artistic and technological, material and teleological, efficient and formal

3) a means of modifying the environment and a method of organizing the self, the making of art and music and poetry, the fashioning of memory and history and philosophy, the construction of perception and expression and reality

4) an independent publisher with a steadfast goal to print and promote outstanding poets, writers and artists that reflect the creative drive and spirit of the new electronic landscape

NeoPoiesisPress.com

www.ingramcontent.com/pod-product-compliance
Lightning Source LLC
LaVergne TN
LVHW021118080426
835509LV00021B/3443